# Sergei
# RACHMANINOFF

## PIANO CONCERTO
## NO. 3

### Op. 30

Study Score
Partitur

PETRUCCI LIBRARY PRESS

# ORCHESTRA

2 Flutes

2 Oboes

2 Clarinets

2 Bassoons

4 Horns

2 Trumpets

3 Trombones

Tuba

Timpani

Percussion
(Side Drum, Bass Drum, Cymbals)

Violins I

Violins II

Violas

Violoncellos

Double Basses

Duration: ca. 40 minutes

First performance
November 28, 1909, New York
Sergei Rachmaninoff, piano solo
New York Symphony / Walter Damrosch

ISBN: 978-1-60874-057-4
This score is a slightly modified unabridged reprint of the score
issued in Moscow by Muzgiz sometime after the composer's death
The score has been scaled to fit the present format.

Printed in the USA
First Printing: January, 2012

*To Josef Hofmann*

# Piano Concerto No. 3
## Op. 30

# I

Sergei Rachmaninoff
(1873–1943)

6

10

40574

14

21

40574

22

26

30

40574

42

40574

44

# II
# Intermezzo

60

40574

62

69

40574

# III
# Finale

78

40574

98

40574

102

40574

40574

122

40574

124

40574

130

40574

6×9

Made in the USA
Middletown, DE
09 October 2018